What Was and Will Be

What Was and Will Be

Eric Chiles

RESOURCE *Publications* · Eugene, Oregon

WHAT WAS AND WILL BE

Resource Publications
An Imprint of Wipf and Stock Publishers
199 W. 8th Ave., Suite 3
Eugene, OR 97401

www.wipfandstock.com

PAPERBACK ISBN: 979-8-3852-2582-8
HARDCOVER ISBN: 979-8-3852-2583-5
EBOOK ISBN: 979-8-3852-2584-2

VERSION NUMBER 07/23/24

For Franklin J. Chiles
1923–2013
"one tough old dude"

Contents

III

IV

I

Herpetology

Their onion skin sheddings laced
in the stone wall betrayed them,
fascinated me. They had eye bubbles.

Perhaps it was the idea of slipping
off skin like clothes, becoming new
and clean rather than slimy
like everyone thought. Yellow-striped
garter snakes—named for something
that held up stockings—coppery milk
snakes which legend said would
steal a sip from a cow's udder.

The scales of indigo racers, shiny as coal,
and rat snakes whispered escape
through the tall grass and leaves,
synchronized ribs running
to all the wood's hidden places.

I would catch them when I could,
hold the crook of a stick on their necks,
and then pinch behind their jaws
with thumb and finger while
their tails wrapped my wrist
in a Cleopatra bracelet, their forked
tongues tasting the air, round eyes
unblinking.

Mostly I caught garter snakes,
put them in the window well that lit
the cellar steps, fed them scraps,
watched them writhe up
the window screen until
Mom made me set them free.

What else lived deep within
the garden's stone wall?

Holy water

It was my father's new Chevrolet
four-door station wagon—two-tone
green. He was so proud of that car
he stenciled the business name
on the dark green front doors
in silver paint—

>   Chiles & Sillivan
>   Contractors

I remember the sun glazing
the brick of Sacred Heart Church
yellow while he finished his
conversation with the red-faced,
white-haired pastor about the job,
absent-mindedly pushing the door
shut on my five-year-old hand.

I screamed. Everything grew blurry
and red. My dad stepped back
as the pastor pulled a small plastic
bottle from under his black cassock
and spritzed some holy water
on my hand, mumbling in Latin,
my tears distorting his face.

And I still wonder if he expected
a miracle.

Salve Regina

The nuns marched us into the pews
for weekly mass. Girls on the left,
boys on the right, grade by grade,
all of us wearing school uniforms.

Cooley and I always managed
to sneak next to one another, and as
sixth graders with two years left
at St. Anne's, we sat near the back.

Once we were all seated in the pews,
Mother Helen Augusta, her red face
florid against her black and white habit
would sternly study her assembly.

Then with the ringing of brass bells,
the mass would begin and Cooley
and I would open our hymnals
ready to join the choir of angels.

Triumph all ye cherubim!
Sing with us ye seraphim!
Heaven and Earth, resound the hymn!
Salve, salve, salve, Regina.

We unleashed our adolescent voices
toward the heavens, unabashed
in our pretended sanctity, ignoring
snickering from the pews behind us.

We weren't singing to impress
seventh and eighth graders, but
Thrones, Dominions, Virtues and
Mother Helen who turned to smile.

Calendar

The foreman's office occupied
the front end of the equipment
trailer, wooden steps leading
to a scavenged door—inside
blueprints on a sawhorse table,
a couple folding chairs, always
a girlie calendar on the wall.

Billy gleamed when he showed
her off. *Wouldn't ya want
a piece of that,* he'd ask, patting
her legs, the name Coleman's
Lumber across the top of June's
thirty days in the year 1966.
Don't the stain give her a nice tan?

Outside, the frame of the bible
church rose from the mud, stacks
of two-by-fours and plywood golden
in the morning sun. It was 9 a.m.
coffee break, and we gathered
to break bread and praise Billy's
handiwork in silent disbelief.

When I decided not to follow my father

I was thirty inches deep and four feet
into a twenty-foot footer
for the addition to the doctor's house,

and the ground was hard,
the air heavy as an obligation,
that cloudy August day.

Each shovelful of dirt
made me sweat doubts.

High school summer help did
the grunt jobs, and that's what
I was even if I was the boss's son.

The trench had to be squared,
so I shaved the clay like finish work.

Perhaps precision would please
the foreman, but the boss showed up
to inspect the job and yelled,

that's not the way, grabbing
the tool from my hands.

He started flinging shovelfuls
like a machine, then, red faced,
held it high—an exclamation point.

That's what I'm paying you to do.
The foreman shook his head.

Joe's whisper

In high school you were always quick
with a wise crack and a smile.
Without a care until
you lost your deferment because
you partied too much and flunked out.
Rather than wait for Uncle Sam to snap
you up, you signed up for Semper Fi.
I remember the night in Obee's garage
when you got back, all of us sipping beer.
There was a shadow in your smile,
things just didn't fit anymore
and late that night you told us
of a search for Vietcong.
In a village you burst
through a hut's door
finding just a frightened woman
clutching a small child.
You froze.
Unsmiling you whispered
that the sergeant yanked you out
and tossed in a grenade.
The night's silence
exploded around us.

Anatomy lessons

The only time I ever shot a pheasant,
my four-year-old daughter wanted

to watch me pluck and gut it out back
in the garage. I worried about nightmares,

but she said she wanted to see how
it was put together—this the tyke who

manhandled our yellow lab, sticking
her hand in his mouth and grabbing

his toothy jaw. He followed her everywhere.
Years later she wanted to tag along with me

on deer hunts, curious about dressing out
something larger, poking entrails and such,

surprised at the size of the animal's heart.
In high school, dissection lab thrilled her,

and by the time she graduated college, she
could look at spots on your nails and ask

pointed questions about your blood pressure.
She knew what was beneath the skin, what

bumps were. When she applied to med school,
the doctors crowed *here's the pheasant girl.*

One Thanksgiving, she called from her surgical
residency excited about her first amputation,

matter of fact about what diabetes can lead to.
I could have used her help carving the turkey.

Beethoven's bust

The boy had perfect pitch;
he could play a scale or chord
after hearing it just once.
Impressed, his middle school teacher
took him aside and coached the gift.
He'd sit next to the boy at the piano,
his hand on his shoulder, tapping time.
The youth responded to the rhythms,
spent hours after school and weekends
with his mentor who assured the parents
their son had talent worth developing.
So they trusted him, allowing sleepovers,
but started to wonder when the man
lavished rewards like a bronzed
plaster of Paris bust of Beethoven
on their prodigy. Then came belligerence,
rumors of pot and beer. Grades
slipped from A's to F's. The student
stopped seeing the teacher, and
the worried parents confided their
concerns in the man. Hoping for
insight, they arranged a meeting
between all parties, but the only
answer was their son's glaring silence
aimed at all three. After dinner
the next day, the son carried the bust
out to the front steps. The father watched
from the front door as the teacher pulled
up to the curb, and his son hurled
Beethoven to the sidewalk.

Cardiac waiting room

—Hospital of the University of Pennsylvania (HUP)

What a time the healthy have while waiting
to hear how the surgeries went. The austere
furniture stresses their discomfort, edging
them into forced conviviality. It's here
health becomes a disability, where it's out
of place, where it's a competition over who
waits for the sickest, where it's about
what dying parents and spouses put them through.
For them patience is a trial whose sentence is
torn magazines, hard chairs, television talk
and complaints about doctors not knowing or his
trouble breathing at night. Except for a silent pair,
his face hard as the chairs, hers white as chalk,
who wait for a child who shouldn't be there.

Unknotted

The weaver's *senneh* knot isn't really tied.
It's a short, colored yarn simply wrapped
around the warp. Good rugs, brightly dyed,
have at least three hundred and twenty packed
into a square inch. It's an open-ended beauty
of millions that fashioned this Tree of Life.

Such an intricate design, such painstaking duty
to detail. Imagine the hours, fingers and knife,
crafting this meditation beneath my feet.

No rug is flawless, there's always an imperfection
woven in as mind and hands work to complete
their task. A drop of sweat causes distraction.

Simplicity is the essence of complexity,
you said. Then you jumped. Knot by knot, I see.

Tattoos I never got

During a hot afternoon game at Yankee Stadium
the young father, son and daughter on either side,
stripped off his shirt. There across his back
in arching letters, scapula to scapula, was his
name, "Davilla," just like the players on the field.
It gave a whole new twist to skins and shirts.
When he turned, on his left pectoral muscle
were two indigo names, son and daughter, probably.
Plenty of room for a growing family which
made me wonder about faithful sons who carry
"Mother" somewhere on their hide. Do daughters
memorialize "Father" that way? There's
a devotional aspect that can't be denied and ink
is another way of testifying to what's written in blood.
Maybe that explains the Marine's "Semper fi."
But how faithful is an abbreviation that sounds
like a cost? What about the old "Death before Dishonor"?
Who will know when the skin grows cold?
What once would bring a proper frown
has become a common expression of individuality,
body art that's less Polynesian tatau and less taboo,
sharp and crisp as the colors in a comic strip,
another kind of blemish that time will fade and blur
until one day the wearer will wonder why.
I've only one sheaf of skin for writing on and it's
for the sun and wind and snow and rain to stain,
for the imprints of your touch and lips, our tears,
your smile whose colors are a more indelible ink.

Photo graph

After looking at an old yearbook photo

I have a photo of this place.
In it, the trees frame your face.

Today it's a simpler view
absent any hint of you.

Where your face was, there's an empty field,
fallow and waiting to be tilled.

I stand where the photographer stood
and take a picture of the field, the wood.

Next to yours it'll plot before and after,
a joke line to coax some hollow laughter.

II

Alchemy

1.

After the steel mill shut down,
the former CFO took us and Charlie,
the venture capitalist, on a tour.
We started in the Welfare Room
where the steelworkers changed
from street clothes using the old-fashioned
pulley-chain buckets instead of lockers.
Steel lath and plaster peeled from the ceiling
of the showers where they washed
off coke grime. Green lottery tickets
littered the floor—tears and lost dreams.

2.

The CFO pitched redevelopment.
At the blast furnaces Charlie recounted
how he took the woman he would wed
on a date there to marvel at the majesty
of manufacturing and endured
our jokes about being a red-hot lover.
Oblivious, in one of the machine shops
he admired the overhead gantry crane,
saying his St. Lawrence boathouse could use it.
His millions couldn't save his missus' mind,
and in despair he put a .32 to their temples.

3.

It took a couple years, but the ex-exec
persuaded the Smithsonian to invest
in an industrial history museum
for the machine shop. When the state
approved casinos, a Las Vegas mogul
bought the ore yard, kept the big ore crane
for a red neon sign, and built a gambling floor
that mimicked the mill with orange ingot
lights hanging from the metal roof trusses.
Folks flock from all over the Northeast,
filling the parking deck to throw away dollars,
and buses arrive hourly from Chinatown
with Chinese eager to cash in vouchers
then snare geese along the Lehigh for dinner.
One plucked his catch in the restroom.

4.

The museum built a walkway along the four
blast furnaces which used to shoot blue
flames into the night when I was a kid.
Last fall my dad's best friend visited
from Phoenix—in his nineties and ailing
—his farewell to his childhood buddy's widow.
We strolled the walkway, the black hulks
of the towering, rusting furnaces to the left,
a derelict ore car to the right, and George
—crooked from time, a 4-F military reject—
told of sweating in the mill during the war,
how workers died in the rush to roll plates
for battleship hulls and forge their cannons.
Trees have sprouted from the stacks,
one clattering gold leaves like clinkers.

Voicemail

If we printed an editorial
criticizing conservatives
on Sunday, I could expect
a flashing red light on my
phone Monday morning.

Always the same slow,
gravelly voice: *Pinko, lefty wacko*
probably never worked a job
where you had to sweat, no idea
what makes America great. Click!

No one else got the voicemails.
Just me probably thanks to our
Memorial Day editorial board
portrait and bios so readers
saw who wrote unsigned opinion.

Sometimes he got personal.
My beard a red-flag proof positive
of radicalism, my glasses evidence
of being an egg head out of touch
with the *real America. Click!*

What was funny was that sometimes
the publisher dictated the editorial,
and as paid scribes we wrote, often
under protest, but that's how
the real America really works.

For a couple years The Voice snuck
out from under his rock to drop
turdy voicemails when he thought
no-one would be there to pick up.
That cowardice was little solace.

I'd let the others hear the messages,
and it became a joke and a game
as we'd try to guess who it was,
try to match The Voice in hope
of having an exchange of views.

Then one Sunday I had to retrieve
something, and the phone rang.
Without picking up, I listened
as the Nameless Voice began to rant.

So I grabbed the receiver demanding,
Who is this? A surprised pause then,
Joe Blow but how'd you know? Click!
And with that the chance for dialogue
died because The Voice never called back.

Peony soup

The management consultant sipped
gazpacho while we supposedly discussed
reorganization, and I remembered

a long ago April before the grape-like buds
of Mom's peony had bloomed. I knew nothing
of botany then, but I knew hurt and jealousy.

One of the neighbors, Glenn, had mocked me
to impress dark-haired Suzy—my first crush
—and she laughed which hurt even more.

I can't remember the taunt, but whatever
five-year-olds know of revenge, I knew then,
as I sulked and plotted down North Street.

I grabbed a galvanized wash tub off the back
porch, poured in water, splashed in some dirt,
and stirred in some peony buds. All I needed

was for my co-conspirator, my little sister,
to lure Glenn to our yard to drool over the soup
while I hid behind a bush ready to clobber him.

The consultant's spoon clattered in his bowl,
and I realized I had hardly heard a word.
At least he picked up the check.

Downsized

Insidious euphemism
hiding so much denial.
It almost sounds
good as in, "I've dropped three
dress sizes" or "I've lost four inches
from my waist."
As in, "I didn't need that boat
of a car. It burned too much gas.
It's so much healthier to ride
a bike everywhere."
As in, "the house was just too big,
all we needed was a two-bedroom flat."
As in clipping coupons, cutting
up credit cards, learning
to say "no," not
answering the phone.
As if that's what you wanted.

Pistol in your lap

Have you ever sat
with a pistol in your lap?

Has your heart and mind
ever had that chat?

Perhaps it was a full
bottle of sleeping pills

or an open oven door,
has that dark chat happened before?

That path diverges two
very different ways.

Don't delude yourself
that one ends in relief.

All it does is cause
someone else's grief.

Anguish was so awful
I couldn't even cry,

but pulling the trigger
would've been a lie.

So, I sat and stared
into the cold blue

then locked it safely
away. A heart beat of hope

had whispered to my mind,
stay, please stay.

Beebe

Years ago my wife and children
wanted to breed our Springer spaniel.
We eventually sold all the litter of eight
except the runt. We named her Beebe.

Her left eye wandered in its socket.
Roscoe, the last brother to leave,
sensing she wasn't right,
would snarl and attack,
biting her neck.
Separating them risked
getting nipped by the savage
pup's needle-like teeth.

Pets mean yellow
puddles on the floor.
But poor Beebe had a
liver and white charm,
a smiling mouth, wagging tail,
that made me pat her head.

Before her first birthday,
she started to limp.
Then she couldn't move
a rear leg. Within a week
she couldn't get up
from her green plaid blanket bed.
The vet found an inoperable
tumor in her spinal cord.

I visited her before she got
the fatal needle.
She lay on a urine-stained
white towel on a cold steel tray.
She could only move
her sad, good eye.
Tearing up, I patted her,
said goodbye and removed
her small red collar.

Now when I go to the garage
to get the lawnmower,
her name tag jingles
from the fading collar hung
on a nail by the door.

Premature

It was way before his time,
fifteen weeks, to be exact,
but who can tell anyone
when to start?

Impatient imp
tried to kick his way out,
so much strength
for someone so small.

Life is always a gift,
but before its time
it's a worry.

Undeveloped
lungs too weak
to breathe
or cry.

Here too soon,
no one was prepared,
not even him.

Fists smaller
than a thumbnail,
frail taut arms
slender enough to slip
dad's wedding band
to his shoulder.

All of a pound
and a half
and twelve
inches long,

but here he is,
ready or not.

Hedge

A long, tall hedge
separates our house
from our neighbor's.
My wife says it provides
some privacy.
I say it's a pain.
She doesn't trim it,
I do—as little as possible.
I'd rather let the damn
thing go wild, or
cut it down, but she
warns, "don't you dare,
the finches nest there."
"Fine," I think, "don't
bother the birds.
Let the bush grow
ragged." But then
the neighbor, a man
of trim compulsion,
cuts the clutter that
intrudes upon his
specified space.
I can take a hint,
so out snakes
the orange extension
cord, the sawtooth
shark of a trimmer,
a finger and cord
menacing machine.

There's the yellow-handled
rake and the warped,
splintered step ladder, too.
Next comes the stretch
of muscles, the sweat,
the pricks of punji
stick branches, the puffs
of choking pollen,
the appliqué of minced
leaves, the red sting
of the summer sun,
the ear numbing
clatter of the ravenous
electric teeth. My wife
and neighbor insulate
themselves in air
conditioned silence.
I rake up the clippings,
stuffing the big black
plastic bag until it
bulges, sharp twigs
poking through. I hate
this hedge. I want to
uproot it. To hell
with privacy
and finches. But
it does look neat.
My wife appears
at the door with a smile
and a glass of lemonade.
"You need a shower."

Wrinkles

After helping my daughter and grandson
out of the car, my son-in-law unloads
two big, black garbage bags of dirty clothes.
Playing with the grandkid has a price.
       Three loads in, the dryer starts clicking
like there's a penny bouncing in the drum.
After the last load, the son-in-law says,
I think the dryer is broken.
                    Well, nothing
lasts forever. In the laundry room, Ryan says,
the drum isn't rotating and pushes on one
of the paddles. Sure enough, it's stuck.
Don't worry, I say, figuring I'll call Sears.
Who fixes things anymore? But my biochemist
son-in-law says, *let's see what's wrong,*
and I realize I've been volunteered to assist
in an experiment.
             So, I help him move
the dryer away from the wall, disconnect
the power cord, and pull off the vent pipe.
Give me a three-eighths socket, he says.
Off comes the galvanized back cover.
You got something for these, Ryan asks, holding
a handful of screws. Into a plastic cup they go.
He shines a light through a tangle of wires.
The pulley came off, he declares, *But we can't
get to it from the back.*

Next we take off the white
enameled top, then the white enameled front,
tilt the dryer backwards, and crack it open
like a clam. I'm thinking I should've called
a repairman, visualizing how old appliances
end up in ditches along back country roads.
But the son-in-law's persistence impresses me.
He's on a mission, and I'm along for the ride,
and I'm beginning to like what I see.
                                                    Of him,
not the dryer. What I see of that is rather
insubstantial.
            Hold the drum steady, he orders,
as he grabs the drive belt, thin as a rubber band.
*Look at all this slack. That pulley must've provided
tension somehow.* Ah, the scientific method at work.
But there's no way to hook the drive belt over
the pulley which is enclosed in its bracket arm.
The thin drive belt is a möbius strip
we need to thread through a twisted nail puzzle.
The son-in-law tries one way, then another.
I try, thinking maybe there's enough bend
in the bracket arm to use it like a spring.
But I'm wrong.
                  I'm committed—I'm starting to sweat.
Hold the drum in place, he orders again,
and he attaches the bracket to its anchor spot,
loops the slack under the pulley, through the bracket,
and over the drive wheel and drum.
                                          It's tight and holds.
I think that's it, Ryan smiles.
We reassemble the dryer, plug it in, turn it on.
It works,
            and I feel really good about the choice
my daughter made.

35

My two wool sweaters

keep me warm.

I bought one from a catalog.
It's camel with a zip turtle neck lined
with fleece and has leather elbow patches.
It cost a lot and was made in China.

The other is a thick gray cable knit
zippered jacket with a hood
and pockets. It came from
a flea market. Its label says
it was made in Ecuador.
It cost twenty dollars.

People always tell me how nice
these sweaters are when I wear them,
and that makes me feel kind
of warm, too.

Then they ask me where
I got them, and that makes
me think.

I wonder where the wool
came from for the one made
in China and how many people
lost jobs in Pennsylvania textile mills.

That doesn't make me worry
too much because the voice
on the other end of the phone
works at a catalog call center
in Minnesota.

But then I think of alpacas
in the Andes, and villagers carding
wool, spindling yarn, knitting the skeins
into sweaters in earthen huts,
sitting around a central fire pit
on rugs laid on dirt floors,
selling five for ten dollars American
to the *yanqui* driving the muddy
Nissan pickup, and then
I feel a chill mountain
draft on my neck.

Our Hall of Fame

The letter didn't come from Canton
or Cooperstown but the principal
of our high school. I had ignored
an earlier email as a gimmick
to open my checkbook, but this
was personally signed, inviting
me and the other members
of our wrestling team, which won
three consecutive state titles,
to a reception and induction
before a basketball game.

Someone had found our trophies
and banners in a closet under
fifty years of debris. A custodian
almost threw them in a dumpster,
but the current coach recognized
a motivational opportunity.

Halls of Fame are serious honors.
They make you remember what
you once had, and their mention
makes obituaries more interesting.

Two thirds of our team showed up,
although, sadly a few had lost life's
last bout. Jude died years ago
from brain cancer. Louie, one of our
lightweights, struggled with sobriety

and succumbed to booze. Mike,
my practice partner, and a college
champ, a children's home director
who consoled my wife and I
during the trials of adolescence
and liked his bourbon on the rocks
despite kidney disease, dropped dead
on the retirement community golf course
while playing a round with his wife.

Bobby, who had defeated an opponent
who later put Slippery Rock on the map
and medaled at the Olympics
became a high-wire ironworker in California,
and our heavyweight, John, who last
I heard was a lobsterman in Maine,
didn't make the trip.

None of us who did come could
make weight today, although, Tim
was closest. He wore the blazer
the school bought us after we won
the second championship in 1966.
I'm sizes past fitting in mine.
He also had a scrap book tracing
all our exploits from CYO through
that last tournament in Lancaster.
What a collection of yellowed memories.

He and Gene talked about operating
cranes at the long-shuttered steel mill.
Jim talked about not being able
to get to the NCAA tournaments
anymore because they're held
on the weekend he opens his

Italian ice stand for the season.
Bruce, who wrestled 106 pounds,
is now as tall as me, the 154 pounder.
Greg who wrestled the weight below
me, and got better every year, drove
up from Virginia where he still
practices law. I hadn't seen him
since graduation, and while we
were competitors then, there
was the sense that night we could
have become better friends.

None of us will ever step on the mat
again and probably won't see each
other before the final fall.

After the Chinese buffet

As my father-in-law and I tick down the highway,
the country western station plays Johnny Horton's

classic about Jackson's sharpshooters slaughtering
all those redcoats as the calendar flipped from 1814 to 1815.

Before the Battle of New Orleans was fought
—such needless bloodshed two weeks after the war's end

—their families had enjoyed a Yule and New Year,
probably joyous about the Treaty of Ghent, unaware

for another month about all those fallen in a swamp,
their separations becoming unhealable wounds.

We chat about the tune on the way to the Chinese buffet,
—no cell phone, left charging at home, to interrupt us

—wondering whether the heat of today's instant word,
not time's lapse, would've cauterized all those gashes.

At the buffet it's pot stickers, sushi, the hibachi grill
and nonagenarian Dorry's flirting with Randi and Yuki.

It's his weekly retreat from watching over his wife,
wheelchair bound and senile, a chance for us

to stay connected before that final hiatus creeping closer,
sharing old hunting stories and grandkid updates.

When I return home, I'm happy to see my son's truck
parked in the drive, glad I haven't missed an opportunity

to extend the sharing with another generation,
only to find him taking care of his mother

who had fallen while standing on a chair,
both angry I hadn't answered their calls.

III

Prophecy

We thought he'd live forever.
He thought so too—and predicted
he'd reach at least 102. He liked
even numbers, half for you,
half for him, no arguments,
except in tennis where he'd crush
a serve to reach 45, having kept
you at love for an entire set.
He was one tough old dude who
had trouble getting matches
in the city B league when he hit
his eighties. No one wanted to play
the frail looking white-haired gramp,
but he'd use finesse and drop
shots to frustrated opponents
decades younger. He wore a T-shirt
with the slogan, *Age and treachery*
beat youth and speed every time.
But the cough wouldn't go away,
and his hack of a doctor misdiagnosed
cancer as persistent bronchitis.
It was like someone trying to break his service,
the set stuck at deuce, so at 88 with
his usual bravado, he had the surgeon
remove 40 percent—nice even number
—of his left lung. To him it was just
another adventure, but rehab was
a bitch, and blowing into the breath
gauge was tougher than dispatching

some sixty-something kid on the court.
Caution shadowed his certainty.
Walking to the mailbox for the daily
conservative cries for his cash
left him breathless. Too much sitting
knotted up his guts. Ironic that an
impacted bowel sent him to the OR
a second time—the guy who preached
intestinal fortitude and bragged
he had never puked and never would.
Now 90, in pre-op he was buoyant,
looking forward to another grudge
match with death, certain his faith
would pull him through. They resected
a length of the duodenum, stuffed
like a sausage, and put in a colostomy port.
The indignity, smell, and staples
zippering shut his gut made his eyes
glower when he demanded a sip of ginger ale.
Instead of burping to release the gas,
he held it in, cheeks bulging, bursting
his stitches. After four agonizing,
drug-dulled days, sepsis killed him.

Pre-dawn calls

Twice you've called when death rang.
The first time you'd been out late
drinking and struck a deer, rumpling
your hood with an unexpected harvest
of venison, and you thought of me,
the unsuccessful hunter who knew
what to do with the crumpled corpse.

So in the dark we dragged it down the field
past the barn, gutted it, and dug a hole
for the offal which in the woods
would've been consumed by crows and coyotes
—but not in the suburbs as the sky grayed.
So perfunctory. What else would one do?
The pulverized meat made a wealth of sausage.

Decades later you dialed me from a hospital
room where you kept watch on our dying
father. This time you waited a respectful
time before informing me, the eldest,
that the expected had transpired
before dawn awakened our world
for everyone except one.

His ties

They still hang on hooks
he screwed into a wardrobe
he salvaged from a dorm room.

He didn't buy any of them new
but at second-hand stores
or estate sales—just like his suits.

He only wore them Sundays,
to baptisms, weddings or funerals.
Otherwise, it was chinos and flannels.

He preferred muted knits
and earth-toned woolen cravats,
a silky stripe for something special.

He favored the asymmetry
of the four-in-hand rather
than a half-Windsor's triangle,

and the crimping of the knots
still crease the ties as they
drape like moth-eaten memories.

Breakfast after church

She needed a ride to mass one Sunday,
so we obliged and were rewarded
by her offer to buy us breakfast.

On the way we passed the mall,
and she recalled those acres were
once a golf course her husband played.

Over coffee and eggs, she remembered
their honeymoon at a Catskill resort
where he tried to teach her the sport.

They made a foursome with some
other honeymooners. She wore loafers
while the others wore their spikes.

On one fairway, she said she swung
nine times at the ball without hitting it.
Embarrassed, she didn't take another stroke.

The next morning, her new spouse
joined the other couple on the tennis court
while she lolled at the lake—alone.

At home, photos of grandchildren bracket
his urn on the mantle, and she muses,
I don't know why I ever stayed with him.

Late blossom

While her husband breathed
she kept her blossoms sheathed.
For big family occasions—like weddings
—she wore simple hand-made fashions
stitched from fabric she bought
at the dollar store, and taught
her daughters how to tailor clothes
—A-line, high-waist, sheath or yoke
—for themselves if the need arose.

For years she wore the same
simple dark blue blouson
until her late's cremation where
she wore a store-bought floral flounce
that made her smile and look so young.
No one ever saw that blue dress again
—she mixed it with his ashes.

His ashes

War makes work for doctors.
Armies need them to repair
warriors for their grim task.

Out of VMI, the Army sent him
to medical school to become
a repairer, and what he saw

—charred flesh, missing limbs,
shrapnel in skulls—scarred him.
Some things can't be fixed while

others can be reused as tools
of training. The selfless sacrifice
of cadavers impressed him most.

WW II ended before his education,
so medical school went unfinished.
But he never forgot the cadavers'

commitment to teach the living,
using up every fiber of their
existence to help others heal.

He did the same, and two years
after his death we interred
his ashes—sandy, drained of lessons.

The orchid garnish

A day of sea air whetted
my wife's lust for fish.

We found a restaurant
overlooking Hyannis Harbor.
As we watched the Nantucket ferries
slide in and out of their berths,
she ordered lobster and scallops.

They come tented in asparagus,
crowned with a vibrantly purple
orchid whose fleshy mouth
is rimmed with an aureola of pink
—a provocative tongue sticking out.

My wife lays the orchid
on the table between us,
then attacks the lobster
with her hands. As she leans
over her plate to stuff succulent
lumps in her mouth, I glimpse
white curves inside her shell
untouched by the sun.

She licks the juices and butter
from her fingers then picks up
the orchid, drapes it over
her ear, flutters negligee
eyelashes, and aims a moonlight
smile. My mouth waters.

Gray baby blues

Bye-bye dye,
women sure do mystify,
they got this urge to beautify,
bye-bye dye, goodbye.

Bye-bye dye,
women can be so sly,
I didn't know that colors lie,
bye-bye dye, goodbye.

Oh, momma, the gray's here to stay,
now don't you hide yourself away.

Bye-bye, dye,
my gal's hair pleased my eye,
always sparkled like the sky,
bye-bye dye, goodbye.

Bye-bye dye,
those sweet tresses made me sigh
made me sweat like July,
bye-bye dye, goodbye.

Oh, pretty baby all I got to say
is your blue eyes hide the gray.

It doesn't get any better than this

The kids are grown and gone
    and don't call for cash.

The roof doesn't leak
    and the furnace keeps us warm.

There's food in the fridge
    and cold beer, too.

There's money in the bank
    and the bills are paid.

There's still hair on the top
    and the joints don't creak.

My honey still loves me
    and doesn't seem to mind the paunch.

The ticker works fine
    and I don't need the blue pill.

The sky is blue, nothing but good days ahead,
    and I just might live forever.

Spring Twilight

At the margin of a spring night so clear
it would define a vacuum, there was nothing
between the house, the lawn and the tree
when she looked out across the backyard
from the kitchen window as she finished
their simple dinner. What a day it had been,
the air so new, fresh and bright
with leaves, sun, sky, grass and birds
breaking forth as if birthed from winter's
womb with eyes that saw everything
for the first time. Even meat and potatoes
would taste like a banquet tonight, elevated
to grandeur by simple salt and pepper,
a touch of greens and a glass of beer.
He put in a CD before they sat at the table,
Gershwin, and by the time they had finished
his fingers kept rhythm to "The Man I Love."
She smiled, her eyes bright with some delight.
She reached for his hand. "Let's dance."
The words touched him unexpectedly
in his reverie. A shell cracked, he made a face
but she squeezed and persisted, "Come on."
Her eyes, those dark eyes, clear and deep
as well water and just as sweet and inviting.
"Come on," the sound of a flower breaking
its green sheath, and his face softened
with a question, "where?" With just a nod
she motioned outside, into the spring twilight
where the last traces of sun still lingered yellow

on the edges of another year's leaves,
green deepened by shadows as the sky slipped
toward night's indigo. It was the first time,
again, and he took her hand like the delicate
thing it had become, as fragile old as it was
new, and followed her out the door into
the dawning of yet another year, another
spring, and he held her close and dear,
listening not just to Gershwin but the wind
of their reborn hearts as their feet stepped
lightly, refreshed through tender, new grass,
beneath the leaves, beneath the waking stars,
in air so fresh the old became new.

Cataracts

Plunging over a cataract,
paddling furiously,
blinking to clear my eyes.

I should've expected
that time's waters would
have the same effect.

So many waves have poured
through those dilated
narrows, so many sights,

that the fern fringed
pools have started to cloud,
blurring the bottom,

spinning my kayak around
in the day's foamy splashes,
the sun becoming a smudge.

IV

AI motivation*

When I used to backpack every summer,
I relied on a digital watch to gauge miles.
Every hour meant I walked two miles or so,
pleased if my pace got me to camp early.
But the watch died. Bad seal, bad battery,
water short circuited the LC display.
Machines wear out, and after not hiking
for a couple years I learned the hard way
that humans do too. My ticker fritzed,
not in a major way, but bad enough
to make me realize my mortality.
After the repairs and rehab came routine
walking three miles along the nature trail
and getting a smart watch with apps like
the one that lets me read my EKG
and another that records my exercise,
minutes, distances, calories and, most vital,
my heart rate which jumps about ten beats
when I go uphill. It's all linked to my
smartphone and the two work in tandem
to keep me on track, so while I'm admiring
the gold finches flash over wild flowers,
the deer browsing, the Monarchs fluttering
milkweed to milkweed, the fox darting across
the path, these two say to one another
digitally—*numbers look good!* And to me,
Keep it up Mom, you can set a record today.

58

(Yes, *Mom*, apparently there are limits
to artificial intelligence—and mine, too,
because I don't know how to fix that.)
And when I get back to the car, no joke,
my watch flashes more encouragement,
Way to go, Mom, you really seized the day.
And I feel motivated, proud, and confused.

* *Something that can happen when you trade cell phones
with your wife.*

Medi-maze

Everyone gets enrolled in Part A,
that's the easy part of turning sixty-five.
It's choosing Parts B, C, and D that dismays.

You thought retirement meant easy days?
But you need a supplemental plan to survive
even though everyone gets Part A.

Consider carefully the donut hole and copays.
I'd rather watch grandkids. When do they arrive?
(Warning: Choose Part B without delay.)

It's enough to make your gray get gray.
Parts F, G, K, L, M, and N? Man alive!
At least you're enrolled in Part A

because that'll pay for your hospital stay.
Insurers and bureaucrats sure connive
to make choosing all those parts a maze.

Cheer up. Next year it will all replay
in October with more confusing jive.
Don't worry, everyone gets Part A.
Choosing Parts B, C, D, et al will dismay.

Graduated

"Just one word . . . plastics."
—MR. MCGUIRE IN "THE GRADUATE"

Benjamin Braddock, in a way, took the advice.
When he and Elaine settled into their nice
California bungalow, they furnished it
with their MasterCharge, and when the kids
came along, Visa also kept their American Dream
afloat at birthdays, holidays, vacations, college,
and everything else they wanted, even their
retirement which they spent sliding player's
club cards into the slot machines at the casino
until the bank Elaine's father founded foreclosed
on the bungalow and wheel chairs and strokes
persuaded the kids to shuttle Ben and Elaine
off to some cheap assisted living complex where
they listened endlessly to Simon & Garfunkel
sing about Joe DiMaggio—woe, woe, woe.

Hospital time

Somewhere between birth
and departure there's
a place where seconds
stretch and an hour
becomes all day.
It's filled with forms
and green lines going up
and down
on a black computer screen
that stands on a tripod with wheels
and has yards of cords and tubes
running to a bed. Everyday
life stops
for nurses and X-rays,
waiting and waiting for a doctor
to diagnose the pain and
never showing up.

When parents become

When parents become
children,
we scold them if they forget
to take their pills.
We patiently listen as they rail,
rheumy eyes bulging,
about what's wrong with the world,
pretending that their words
make sense,
then dab the drool from their chins,
glad the tantrum has passed.

When parents become
children,
we spoon broth past toothless gums,
brush their hair,
change their beds.
We hold their hands as they nod off
to that endless sleep,
feeling abandoned
like children.

Wiggy

The last time we talked, he wanted
me to take a stack of fly fishing magazines.
It was one among many purposefully
piled in his living room. *National Geographics,*
Golf Digests, Wall Street Journals, each
a pier of obligation arranged like obelisks
whose hieroglyphs he must one day decipher.
He found my offer to recycle them
appalling. *What? You're a journalist!*
How could you toss all that information?

He was an older cousin who'd pop in
and out of our lives to remind
us of some curious bit of family
history—a bachelor who occupied
his parents' memory-filled house.
Occupied—not lived there. He might
not have been married, but he stayed
with another cousin's widow.
He didn't want the rest of us
to know he was *living in sin.*

The sin was that we didn't know
him better. One day his companion
called to say she found him collapsed
among the stacks, lifeless as yellow pages.
Weeks later we sorted through boxes
of his black and white family photos
from decades past. *There's Aunt Ruth,*
Uncle Ted. Where's this? Who's that?

He had always been the compass rose
of our family map, the pointer
to things ancestral where secrets hid.
As apparitions multiplied, we slowly grasped
how lost we were in losing him.

Angelus

In the quickening dusk of her mother's
death, the daughter deals as she can.
For years, dementia kept the old woman
from housekeeping, and her father
cooked all the meals in a frying pan.

Distracted, the daughter sees how years
of dust and cooking grease have yellowed
lace curtains embroidered with grape vines,
clouding the setting sun as the nurse doses
morphine to ease the dying woman's coughs.

She unhooks curtain rods, slides sheers
into a pile that shrouds the kitchen floor.
If nothing else, at least she can do this.
Silent, her father stares at a half empty plate
then asks her to help him into bed.

All night she washes, irons, and folds,
busy work to push the coughing out of mind.
She trashes venetian blinds beyond redemption.
She holds vigil through the dark, wiping off sills,
Windexing windows, the coughs subsiding

like a tide as she rinses her wash cloth
in the sink. The angelus of dawn birdsong
echoes through the glass as she slides the sheers
into place, brews coffee, holds her cup like
a chalice as day lights the dossal in dead quiet.

Piano bench

The only music we ever heard
was the symphony of voices during
Sunday family pasta dinners, clinking
dishes in the sink, cabinet doors slapping shut.

So, the piano and bench posed a question
for years in the living room. Who sat
there to play? Instead, they got piled
with books, picture frames, flower vases.

It wasn't until the old lady passed
and her grandson hauled both of them
away that the piano bench divulged
its secret—scores of music she once played.

Long ago in the dusty past her fingers
danced waltzes on the keys. Her smile
lingered in the pages at odds with the dour
duty of feeding husband and family.

There was a different gaiety once in that house,
not that there wasn't laughter all those Sundays,
but something she enjoyed enough to learn
was stored away and forgotten in that bench.

Until it was moved, the lid flopping open
in the bed of the truck, and the wind picking
up the yellowed sheet music, scattering it across
the lawn, golden leaves from the family tree.

Time capsule

The twenty-gallon glass water jug
stood in a corner of the bedroom
closet, its shoulders coated with dust.

Hefty with coins, it was hard to move
into the light. When we wiped it
off, it sparkled with copper and silver.

How many years did it take him
to save all this, a handful of change
scooped from work pants at day's end?

Pennies, nickels and dimes left over
from buying sand or cement or bricks
or gas held in his lime-chapped palms,

an unexpected bequest not mentioned
in the will, so heavy we couldn't pick it
up, so we tipped it so it wouldn't shatter

and poured out a treasure tide tinkling
like the chimes of an old alarm clock.
There's a 1918 Wheat penny, a grimy

Mercury dime, a Standing Liberty quarter
date worn off by decades of fingers,
a Buffalo nickel in the same decline.

Even a chip of mortar. Years of frugality,
saving what he could without a word,
a time capsule of more than small change.

Duck eggs

The ducklings would start to appear
two months after Easter. More mess
than cuteness by then, families
abandoned them in Monocacy Park.
By summer's end, flotillas of white
would raft the creek's rapids.

Uneducated orphans, the ducks didn't
know how to nest, so when the eggs
came, they dropped them in the cool
waters where they stood out like alabaster
pebbles. My father, with hungry mouths
to feed, recognized a welcomed bounty.

If the ducks didn't know how to nest,
my parents did. There were eight of us
by then, a ravenous rabble gobbling up
whatever my mother set on the table.
So my father started wading the creek
collecting the chilled eggs.

Most of us feasted on scrambled
duck eggs, pumpkin rolls and cakes
all enriched with dark orange yolks.
Except me. Eggs were supposed to come
from chickens and in a box bought
at the grocery store. Not a dirty creek.

So while my siblings giggled over
Mom's gooey chocolate gobs, I glared
wondering why she wouldn't use
store-bought eggs. What foolishness
I realize, as I whisk some from the coop
for this ham and cheese omelet.

Jam time

Somewhere between beating
the birds to the raspberry bushes
along the alley behind the house
and morning coffee, I remember
Grammy Concilio's grape arbor.
Concords. Chewy skins in her jam.

I didn't trust anything homemade
as a child after Granddad scared
me away from tapioca pudding
when he told me it was made from
a root whose bark was poisonous.
Only five, my bowl unfinished forever.

If food was in a can or a box or wrapped
on a store shelf, it must be safe
little me reasoned. I wouldn't eat
Mom's gooey chocolate gobs because
she beat in duck eggs Dad plucked
from Monocacy Creek's cold waters.

But I have two cups of fresh raspberries,
—and scratches on my knuckles—
to add to the two I picked yesterday,
and these scarlet gems spoil
almost as quickly as dew dries.
Time to cook the season's first batch.

Tomorrow morning I'll paint
a toasted English muffin red
with fresh raspberry jam, enjoying
it with my coffee, watching the sun
through the window trace their
faces across the tablecloth.

Baby fat

A cardinal comets
across the yard ferrying
a grub for its hatchlings
while my fingers squeeze
my grandson's chubby
thighs, his fat feet pushing
up my lap, knees and ankles
dimpled by that smooth
soft layer that feeds
his hungry brain as it
digests all his sky
blue eyes gobble, sounds
draining into his ears
as he grabs my beard
and peels back the veil
of memory, PopPop
kneading my infant legs
with his proud hands as
strawberry blond strands
waft in the past's wind,
cooing into my ear
whispers of dreams I can
only hear through my own
voice as I hold this rollypolly
potential whose attention
catches a dragonfly cruise
above sun sparkled grass,

the chirr of katydids
in the tall tulip poplars,
the echoes of all
that was and will be.

Acknowledgements

Poems in this collection have appeared
in the following journals:

Allegro—Beethoven's bust, Premature, The orchid garnish

Apeiron Review—Pre-dawn calls

Blue Collar Review—Alchemy, Voice mail, When I decided not
to follow my father

Blue Mountain Review—Herpetology

Chiron Review—Downsized, Gray baby blues, Hedge, His ashes,
Hospital time, It doesn't get any better than this, Spring twilight,
Tattoos I never got

Flying Island—Duck eggs, Piano bench

Gravel—Anatomy lessons

Hidden Oak—Photo graph

I-70 Review—Peony soup

Main Street Rag—Wrinkles

Mobius—My two wool sweaters

Paterson Literary Review—Wiggy

Pembroke Magazine—Unknotted

Pennsylvania English—His ties, Holy water

Plainsongs—Joe's whisper

Quiet Diamonds—Baby fat

Rattle—Medi-maze

San Pedro River Review—Cardiac waiting room

Smoky Blue Literary and Arts Magazine—Breakfast after church

Sport Literate—Our Hall of Fame

Tar River Poetry—Graduated

The American Journal of Poetry—Late blossom, Prophecy

The Comstock Review—After the Chinese buffet

The Dead Pets Poetry Anthology—Beebe

Third Wednesday—Angelus, Time capsule, When parents become

Tipton Poetry Journal—Salve Regina

West Texas Literary Review—Calendar

Word Fountain—Jam time

Cataracts, Jam Time, Spring Twilight, and *The orchid garnish* also appeared in the chapbook *"Caught in Between"* published by Desert Willow Press (2019).

The orchid garnish won the 2015 Cape Cod Writers' Center Poetry Contest. *Baby fat* was an Honorable Mention in the 2022 issue of Quiet Diamonds. *Joe's whisper* was an Award Poem in the Spring/Summer 2023 issue of Plainsongs. *Wiggy* was an Honorable Mention in the 2023 Allen Ginsburg Poetry Awards of the Poetry Center of Passaic County Community College.

www.ingramcontent.com/pod-product-compliance
Lightning Source LLC
Chambersburg PA
CBHW070827100426
42813CB00003B/521